Enabling The Human Spirit: The J.E. Hanger Story

Chris Ingraham

Enabling The Human Spirit: The J.E. Hanger Story

Chris Ingraham

Printed in the United States of America

ISBN: 1-891231-98-7

Library of Congress Control Number
2002112624

Word Association Publishers
205 Fifth Avenue
Tarentum, Pennsylvania 15084
1-800-827-7903
www.wordassociation.com

Foreword

The legacy of J.E. Hanger is a tremendous inspiration not just to amputees, but to all people. This book illustrates the amazing ability of our inner strength when challenge strikes in our lives, and the miraculous accomplishments we can achieve if we believe in the power of the human spirit.

Ivan R. Sabel
Hanger Orthopedic Group, Inc.
Chairman of the Board and
Chief Executive Officer

Enabling the Human Spirit

Alaska's Mt. McKinley has the highest peak on the North American continent, and Ed Hommer stands at the summit, resting after his ascent. A sturdiness to his stance bespeaks a man not easily deterred from his goals. In this, his moment of accomplishment, he fixes his eyes over the white folds of earth that spread over the distant expanse, and sighs. The rigor to his gaze and the depth of his thoughts convey a world of emotion welling behind the stoic facade. Ed has come a long way, and now he knows something important.

Brian Frasure stands on a damp track in Sydney, Australia, battered by the rain. His chest heaves in and out beneath the number pinned on his racing jersey. The scoreboard posts 11.33 seconds, and the crowd erupts. This time marks within a second of the 100-meter dash world record. Brian raises a sure hand in triumph. He knows.

In mid-air, the silence has no comparison. Dana Bowman falls, listening, from an airplane that dropped him several thousand feet over ground. Beneath him the everyday world approaches, but he measures his life in this air, this space between the everyday and the extraordinary. Dana pulls the ripcord. The parachute flies open. His feet hit safely on land, and unperturbed, he walks away. The immediate speed of his step, and the grace with which he disrobes his chute, both reveal a certain confidence. This man knows something, too.

Dana Bowman continues to skydive following a terrible accident that cost him his legs. He now uses two specially designed prosthetic legs that enable him to continue participating in the sport he loves.

What Ed knows from the summit, what Brian knows from the track, and what Dana knows as he finishes a successful jump, is all the same. They know the power of the human spirit. They know it because they have faced one of life's most handicapping misfortunes, and refused to be slowed down.

Each of these three men has lost one or both of his natural legs. More importantly, they overcame their losses, thanks to superior artificial limbs made and fit by Hanger Prosthetics & Orthotics, Inc.– the world's leading provider and manufacturer of prosthetic limbs and orthopedic appliances.

For decades, Hanger Prosthetics & Orthotics has helped amputees overcome the difficulties associated with limb loss. The company is founded on principles of goodwill, perseverance, humanitarianism and innovation. Hanger is a winner. That is why, more than 100 years after its formation, Hanger points Ed Hommer toward the summit; Hanger assists Brian Frasure to world-record speeds; and Hanger guides Dana Bowman to a safe landing.

As amazing as their stories are, none would be possible if not for another man's equally impressive story. It is the story of James Edward Hanger, founder of Hanger Prosthetics & Orthotics. Follow along on a journey into the heart of innovation and perseverance; explore the heart of Hanger.

Company founder James Edward Hanger

James Hanger:
First Amputee of the Civil War

A torrential rain bears down on the rolling hills of old Virginia. It hardly falls at all, this rain, but hangs there instead like a thickness added to the air, or like bubbles shooting through water. The year is 1861. Young James Hanger rides his horse along the Staunton-Parkersburg turnpike, westward over the Alleghenies. Mud splatters the horse's skinny legs at every step. James' legs, dangling on either side, are also mud caked, but strong. They course with blood and virility. He heads to western Virginia, eager to put those legs to work for the Confederate Army in a small town called Philippi.

James left home once before, but this time is different. For the first departure, two years earlier at age sixteen, James left his family's home in Churchville, Virginia to attend Washington College in Lexington. College enthralled him; he was happy studying mechanical engineering at what is now Washington and Lee University. But America was at unrest. A Civil War was sprouting between the North and the South, and after his sophomore year, James returned to Churchville with hopes to enlist in the war on behalf of the Confederacy.

Naturally, James' parents opposed the plan. His father, William Alexander, owned a plantation in Mt. Hope, Virginia, where James was born on February 25, 1843. William Alexander and his wife, Eliza Hogshead, supported the Confederacy, but hoped their young son would stay behind. James' mother told him she would rather he stayed home than leave to fight in what may become a dangerous war. Besides, she thought, he was doing well in his studies and that ought to take priority. Nonetheless, James bristled with determination to answer his call to arms. He figured he would always have the chance to apply his education later. Little did he know that chance would come sooner than he anticipated.

Before long, James' mother realized her son was compelled to enlist. She advised that if he insisted on leaving, he might at least consider joining the local Churchville cavalry, in which two of his brothers were already enlisted under Confederate Colonel George A. Porterfield. The idea made as much sense as any. With that, James took the food and clothing his mother sent with him to give his brothers, and headed west to meet them in Philippi, where their company was stationed.

This was late in May, 1861. The war then was hardly even a war. Rumors filtered down mainly of quiet times by campfire, rolling dice and waiting. Mystery shrouded the events of the war ahead like the rainy haze that obscured his path westward. What the future held he could not tell. He knew only of his willingness to fight. And while deep inside, James must have prepared himself to face anything, he could hardly have prepared for what all lay ahead.

Strategically, springtime of 1861 signified an important time for the beginning of the Civil War. In mid-May, Confederate General Robert E. Lee ordered Colonel Porterfield to Grafton, Virginia, where Porterfield was expected to meet and command 5,000 waiting Confederate enlistees. Porterfield's campaign was to use the 5,000 men to capture and hold 205 miles of the strategically valuable Baltimore & Ohio Railroad, from Wheeling in the north, to Parkersburg in the southwest.

On May fourteenth, Colonel Porterfield arrived in Grafton as planned, but to great surprise, he found the people of western Virginia unenthusiastic about taking arms for the Confederacy. The numbers were nowhere near 5,000. Volunteers were few and equipment scarce. The few Confederate supporters who were present advised Porterfield that he might try Philippi, sixteen miles to the south, as there were thought to be Confederate enlistees encamped there. Without much choice, Porterfield decided to journey toward Philippi and recruit more soldiers.

To the colonel's dismay, in Philippi, Porterfield did not find the mass of men he expected. Most of those present were young, unarmed country-folk, the majority of whom belonged to the Upshur County cavalry. The Upshur men stood by their taut white military tents, proud and erect, looking quite spiffy and ready for action, but they could claim not one weapon among them. Porterfield's efforts to train the ill-equipped troops became futile; and, eventually, he sent many of the soldiers home. He opted to retain only the Upshur cavalry, primarily because their new tents afforded such an impressive military display. After the discouraged companies departed, no more than 400 soldiers remained under Porterfield's command. These numbers posed little threat to the Union troops, particularly given the Confederacy's paucity of weapons. Porterfield waited for more weapons and troops to arrive, but delivery only supplied useless rusted rifles and cartridges, whose size made them unusable with the available artillery.

Despite the inadequacy of his forces, Virginia Governor John Letcher ordered Colonel Porterfield to seize a train and proceed to Wheeling, where he was to capture a large supply of Federal arms. Porterfield delayed action as long as possible, still waiting for reinforcements to arrive. When none did, he decided that the seizure of Wheeling would be too risky. Wheeling was pro-Union and home to a strong force of Union soldiers, under the command of Colonel Benjamin F. Kelley. Overriding the governor's command, Porterfield instead sent a group of men to burn two important bridges situated along the Baltimore & Ohio Railroad, west and northwest of Grafton. After that he returned to Philippi, where James Hanger arrived late at night on June first.

Immediately upon arriving, James inquired about his brothers. Locals told him that the older Hanger brothers had left that night with their company, headed for Buckhannon, and would return tomorrow. James at once declared his intentions to enlist among the Churchville cavalry. The townsfolk wasted no time in accommodating the rookie volunteer as best they could. They guided him to Garrett Johnson's barn, a lodging-house for the remaining boys from the Churchville cavalry. By then it was late, or real early, and James' journey had been tiresome. He found a nice place to sleep in the loft, using hay as a mattress. His horse slept in the stable below.

When he awoke, the sky was clear and the valley's Sunday morning quiet brought a peaceful tranquility to the small town. Philippi nestled cozily in the Tygart River Valley of what is now West Virginia's Barbour County. Hardwood trees carpeted the terrain with dense and damp hillsides. The Tygart River cut through the town, hugging the green hump of earth rising to the city's west, and curving out through the valley's far end. James explored his new, if only temporary home.

Soon he met a cluster of the Confederate volunteers who had come during Porterfield's absence in Grafton. Their numbers added to the 400 already enlisted under Porterfield, and pushed the soldier count to nearly 750. It was an improvement, but still not much. James and the others whiled away the hours without much concern, waiting for Colonel Porterfield to give his next order.

Meanwhile, Union troops mobilized. When Porterfield had ordered the high-traffic bridges burned instead of overpowering the train and attacking Wheeling, Union Major General George B. McClellan perceived this as an act of war. As soon as word of the vandalism reached Camp Denison, where McClellan was stationed near Cincinnati, McClellan ordered Union Colonel Kelley to repair the bridges and advance toward Grafton to avenge Porterfield's act. McClellan also commanded other Union Colonels from surrounding areas to follow in suit.

On June first, the same night James Hanger arrived in Philippi, Colonel Kelley reached Grafton, where he awaited the arrival of Brig. General Thomas A. Morris, whom McClellan had placed in charge of the Union's western Virginia campaign. When Morris arrived in Grafton that night, he devised his plan. The Union would attack Philippi with a pincer method, surrounding it on all sides. They would use two columns of troops to approach from the north, and a third to cut off a possible Confederate retreat along the Beverly-Fairmont turnpike to the south. The complications of the plan would take time to resolve, and despite Kelley's enthusiasm to march onward, Morris decided to delay action another day to finalize details and make the crucial commands.

This all happened unbeknownst to the troops in Philippi. However, during James Hanger's first afternoon in town, startling news arrived of the Union's plans. Two ladies from Fairmont and Pruntytown, small villages near Grafton, brought word that Federal forces 4,500 strong were planning a march on Philippi in three columns, and were expected to arrive sometime that night. Hanger would recall, "This report as a matter of course threw the town and camp into a state of terrible excitement." Indeed, almost immediately the town and camp brimmed with an apprehension marked not so much by fear as by uncertainty. No one could dispute the report of the two ladies, who were quite obviously agitated after having fled from their own towns when Federal forces passed through not long before. But no one knew what to do.

Afraid of the immensity of the opposition's force, Colonel Porterfield ordered his troops to pack up and be prepared to leave at a moment's notice. Poor James had just barely arrived. The town bustled to action. Horses were fed; clothing bundled; pots were boxed. Only the tents from the Upshur cavalry remained as a bold pretense of power. The small town that had swollen with the buzz and belongings of several hundred soldiers sunk down like a sponge drying of its water.

At nightfall, Colonel Porterfield announced that they would not move until midnight. All troops were prepared to flee the Federal opposition by retreating to a town called Beverly, 40 miles to the south. The wait until midnight sent Confederate nerves wobbling. A silent chill spilled over Philippi.

Back in Grafton, the Union men proceeded on their course with dutiful obedience. Two of the three dispatched columns met as planned in a town called Webster, shortly before midnight. They were on pace to reach Philippi and engage battle as scheduled, by 4:00 a.m.

Around midnight, the skies covering western Virginia began to rain, and the rain fell hard and continuously through the darkness. In Philippi, midnight passed and Porterfield still had not given the command to move out. He knew that the advancing groups of Union soldiers were vastly more powerful than his own. After all, his entire assembly of troops in Philippi was still mostly untrained and unarmed. The addition of Churchville's cavalry had helped a little, but not considerably. They still did not possess a single cartridge for battle, but had only loose powder, ball and shot. Despite the Confederate troops' obvious vulnerability, Porterfield made no orders to depart. In all likelihood, he thought no enemy would dare march forward under such difficult conditions—in these days, darkness and rain were truly formidable obstacles. So night grew old, the rain continued, and his men stayed put.

James Hanger slept in the Garrett Johnson barn as he had the night before. Others bunked in the town courthouse, in vacant buildings and in private homes. The Upshur cavalry slept proudly in their new tents. Hanger and the others in the barn were lively despite the cold and the circumstances. They jumped and pulled themselves into the loft with great strength and agility. Nestled above the stable that housed their horses, they could rest safely for the night while picket guards watched for danger on the town's perimeter.

But outside where the pickets watched, the rain grew worse. A cape drew over the sky and covered the stars. The earth slopped with mud, and the river rose. On the edge of town, where the pickets scouted, no shelter covered them from the downpour. Wetness ruled the night. Colonel Porterfield had already allowed his officers to settle in for a night's rest. Motionless, Philippi slept. The rain pattered its monotonous droll outside, and the pickets watched into the darkness. Nothing stirred. Mud splat upward from the ground with every drop of rain that had not already caught and pelted their bodies. Discouraged by the rain, the pickets left their stations to seek shelter, and to sleep like the others.

With Philippi unguarded and asleep, the Federal forces converged safely above the town on Talbott's Hill. Although their journey had been slow and darkness had blinded their vision beyond just a few feet ahead, both columns arrived as planned. They were exhausted from their long trek, a trip that had carried them over rough terrain and rugged roads that often washed away with mud and rain. But exhaustion aside, they were ready to attack.

A battery of cannons, equipped with six-pound balls, craned their necks toward the town below. No one was allowed to fire from the battery until the third column arrived in place to impede a Rebel retreat. The attack signal would be a pistol shot, sometime around daybreak, and then the men on Talbott's Hill were expected to launch cannon balls that would begin the Civil War's first battle on land.

Up on Talbott's Hill not everything went according to plan. The 4,500 uniformed men awaited word of the third column's arrival at the southern flank, but their sheer size made it impossible to remain inconspicuous. Mrs. Thomas Humphreys, a woman sleeping in her home near the top of the hill, not two miles outside Philippi, heard the commotion from their arrival and awoke from her slumber. As a Confederate supporter, she quickly roused her son and sent him ahead to deliver the news to Philippi, by horseback. Before he could make it to town, however, Union officers captured the young man. When Mrs. Humphreys saw her son had been captured, she grew infuriated, and drew a gun. Confusion ensued. Whether the soldiers made a move forward, or whether Mrs. Humphreys was startled will never be known, but her gun fired and sent a rattling boom echoing through the valley.

The natural seclusion of Philippi and the lack of industrialization during that time in history made even the slightest noise stand out for miles. The first shot of the first land battle of the Civil War had been fired by a civilian bystander. Mrs. Humphreys' gunshot roused the sleeping town below, and for the poised Federal soldiers, it played like a trumpet sounding their initial charge into battle. The men controlling the battery of cannons took the noise for the official signal, and commenced their attack. The offensive certainly caught the Confederates off guard, and the battle began prematurely, for the Union's third column had still not arrived to block a Confederate retreat. General Morris' careful plans went awry, as explosions boomed, and the sleeping sprung from their beds.

James Hanger, as the newest enlistee, was on patrol-guard duty immediately outside the barn when the commotion began.   The first two cannon shots thundered from their canisters, and thick clouds of smoke emerged atop Talbott's Hill. The cannonballs sailed through the early morning air to crash among the rain trodden tents of the Upshur grays. Hanger retreated into the barn, where the others bustled about already prepared to flee.   The adrenaline and fear of battle spoiled through young Hanger's toes, up the invigorated musculature of his legs, and bolted through his torso.   Another explosion sounded from atop the hill. James grabbed the bag that carried his belongings and turned to mount his horse. His comrades rushed ahead of him and were on their way out of the barn when a wall exploded inward, sending shards of rain-soaked wood to settle on the hay. A resolute, black sphere centered the collision and buffeted through the six planks of oak wall, too suddenly for reaction.   It struck the earth with force and ricocheted upward, still spinning uncontrollably at high speed.   James

Hanger had his leg positioned to enter the foot strap and mount his steed, but the flying cannonball continued its reckless course and James teetered from an agonizing volt. The others were too far off to return. The black whorl fell motionless. Hanger's pain escalated immediately, hammering through his lower half with an intensity he had never known. A six-pound cannonball had shattered his leg.

A Brief History of Amputation

In the modern day, over 75,000 patients undergo lower extremity amputations each year. More than 75 percent of these patients are over age 50, and their reasons for amputation range from accidental injuries or potentially life-threatening diseases, to congenital anomalies. The first real influx of amputations in America, however, resulted from the Civil War. From James Hanger's injury in 1861 to the end of the War in 1865, America saw some 60,000 amputations. Although that may seem like a small figure for a four-year period compared with current figures, keep in mind that before the War, and before modern industrialization, amputation rarely occurred at all. James Hanger was the first of the unfortunate masses to lose a limb in the War's brutal destruction. The pain associated with such loss, even from as far back as 1861, still resonates among amputees today.

There may be nothing we take for granted so much as our ability to maneuver and function with the sensory-motor skills mastered by our arms, hands, legs and feet. They service how we walk, how we brush our teeth in the morning, how we perform those thoughtless gestures of existence as simple as standing up out of a chair. To live with all natural limbs and then have one deprived can often make amputees feel incomplete, both physically and mentally. For some, the deprivation of physical symmetry spawns insecurity and engenders a sensation of failure at constantly having to struggle to execute the mundane activities of everyday life. Others have been able to face amputation and accept its challenges and rewards. In either case, the impairment of bodily function is a serious issue, and, as might be expected, different people cope with it in different ways.

The decision to amputate comes embroidered with difficulty. Most people find the thought of amputating a limb terribly unappealing. Few medical operations yield such blatantly visible results. Losing a natural limb involves a finality most potential amputees are not prepared to face, and the process involved in deciding whether to amputate can often be arduous and agonizing. In some cases the decision is made by a doctor's medical obligations to react appropriately in emergency situations. In non-emergency situations, though, the deliberation could be endless. Amputate? Not amputate? Among the many decisive factors, acceptance and a positive outlook are important in making a sound decision.

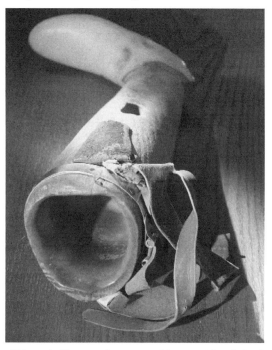

When James Edward Hanger began making artificial limbs, they were carved from wood and fit to the amputee using leather belts and straps.

Historically, amputation slowly evolved from being considered a destructive procedure to being considered a reconstructive one. With limited prosthetic options available to amputees for thousands of years, there was no choice but to consider it entirely destructive. The first written record of prostheses is found in a sacred poem from India called the *Rig Veda*, written between 3500 and 1800 BC. The poem tells of a warrior, Queen Vishpla, who, having lost her leg in battle, was then fitted with an iron prosthesis so she could return to fight. Imagine wearing a leg made of solid iron. Other reports from ancient cultures reveal such a negative attitude toward amputation that some cultures, like the Moche culture of Peru, used amputation as judicial punishment. Theft, for instance, was punishable with the amputation of a hand, laziness with removal of a foot and rebellion with loss of both arms. Even with the birth of science in great civilizations like Egypt, Greece or Rome, prosthetic technology could offer little more than a wooden peg leg attached to the residual limb with a leather cup. Remarkably, it remained this way for thousands of years, until 1861, when a cannonball felled James Hanger in that small barn in western Virginia.

Illustrated by Tom Klinedinst

Hanger's Surgery

In Philippi, the rain continued to pour. After a night of travel, the Union soldiers were as wet as if they had submerged in the river. Kelley brought his men into town as planned, though their weapons were too soaked to be much threat. The cannons continued to fire from the hill, and Kelley's troops took shots as best they could. A few Confederate volunteers stood their ground to make a counter-attack, but their numbers were too outmatched, and they shortly fled south as planned.

Back in the barn, Hanger lay on the hay next to shards of splintered wood. Rain leaked through the hole where the cannonball had burst inside to bludgeon his leg. Beneath James dripped a puddle of blood. It stained the hay through like the rain that seeped through the earth outside. The wound pulsed with an agonizing throbbing, and with every new ounce of blood spilled, Hanger's energy waned and weakened. Unable to retreat with the others, James positioned himself in the hay where he could at least stay well hidden. The pain enervated his power to sustain, as blood flowed incessantly, and his faculties drained. In minutes he fell unconscious.

Outside, the pandemonium of battle bordered on chaos. Confederate troops raced toward the southern exit of town, some on horse, others by foot. The sun rose over the wooded hills and the rain relaxed to a steady but light drizzle. Union soldiers seized control of Philippi, much to their surprise, without much difficulty. Back when Porterfield ordered those bridges burned, the Union perceived the affront as indicative of a far greater threat than what the inadequately equipped Confederate force could actually pose. Reports had suggested Porterfield's army was several thousand strong, and there was no cause to doubt it; even General Lee had made an optimistic promise of 5,000 men. But when the Union columns arrived in Philippi to find their opposition's force so meager and feeble, they were pleasantly surprised. The battle was a rout. Reporters from newspapers in the area immediately dubbed the campaign "The Philippi Races," because there was a lot more racing to escape than actual combat.

Four hours after the battle ended, the Union columns gathered the remaining Confederates as prisoners. Most others had escaped on their route toward Beverly without being deterred by the third Union column, whose arrival was delayed by the night's rain and the confrontation's unexpectedly premature beginning. At this point, the Union volunteers raided the town to plunder the spoils of their victory. In doing so, the Sixteenth Ohio Volunteer Infantry Regiment found James Hanger writhing with pain in the barn where he had been maimed by the cannonball. Bugs brought out by the rain had gathered in the barn, and they ignored even the tepid scent of horse manure to fasten instead on Hanger's wound, which had turned raunchy since that morning. Among the Ohio Volunteers was a doctor named James D. Robinson. When Dr. Robinson saw that Hanger's pain was intense and his condition just as devastating, he rolled his shirtsleeves and called out orders.

He would need a table, door, anything at all and quickly! He would have to amputate.

At the time, those words did not carry the same implications as they would years later. On June 3, 1861, the war was young. This attack had been the first land battle, and Dr. Robinson's surgery would be the war's first amputation, as well.

The men followed Dr. Robinson's orders. They

unfastened the barn door from its hinges and set it out across two stacks of hay. Dr. Robinson used the door as a table from which to perform his operation. Hanger slipped in and out of hallucinating consciousness. Loss of blood had nearly spelled his death, when Robinson, leaning over Hanger's decimated leg, began to work.

Even the best medical expertise then wore the curse of inexperience and ineptitude. In the early 1860s it took only two years to become a surgeon. In 1860, only twenty percent of all surgeons had ever participated, even as witnesses, in an amputation. Robinson was not one of them. He knew a few basic principles to use as a guide, and he performed them as best he could.

The basic principles would later be documented by prominent physicians of the day, the preeminent tenet seeming to be that surgeons should be quick to use their scalpel and saw. D.J. Julian Chisolm's "Manual of Military Surgery for the Surgeons of the Confederate States Army," states that "The rule in military surgery is absolute that the amputating knife should immediately follow the condemnation of the limb." Hanger's leg was indeed condemned. Robinson had to act promptly to prevent a death from blood loss and infection. As a doctor named Eric Carver would suggest in a paper on Civil War orthopedic surgery practices, a primary amputation performed within 24 hours after a wound's infliction reduced the high rate of infection and saved lives from septicemia and other dangers. The Federal Sanitary Commission made a report on amputations, advising that in cases of "compound gunshot fractures of the thigh, bullet wounds of the knee joint and similar injuries to the leg . . . in order to save life, the limb must be sacrificed." With these philosophies, the decision to amputate was easy. James would have to surrender his leg.

All experts agreed that the closer the amputation was to the trunk of the body, the greater the risk of death. According to Dr. Carver's statistics for Union soldiers during the War, of 6,300 middle thigh amputees, 46 percent survived. Compare that to a 76 percent survival rate for upper arm amputees, and an even lower survival rate of 12 percent for hip joint amputations, and it is clear that, while common, amputation during the Civil War was hardly the safe and painless procedure it is today. As the first candidate for amputation during the

Civil War, and being treated by an inexperienced physician in unsanitary field conditions, James Hanger was at great risk.

Hanger lay on the makeshift operating table with three men standing over him. Dr. Robinson ordered that the amputation be performed using what was called "the circular technique," in which the skin is incised in a circular shape using crude tools and knives. This technique was the oldest and most widely practiced method of operation. With a gruesome knife that resembled a medieval torture instrument, Robinson cut Hanger's left leg slightly above the damage of the wound, about seven inches above the left knee. The volunteers around him took the soft tissue under the skin and pulled it back so not to let it interfere with the bone or the arteries. They then pinched the arteries tight to prevent the flow of blood, and Robinson proceeded to cut.

The pain Hanger must have experienced throughout the amputation defies conceptualization. Noel Clemmer, Civil War medical historian, said, "The pain Hanger must have felt is inconceivable to us today." He explains that, while powerful anesthetics like ether, chloroform and opium grew popular and prevalent as the War progressed, at the time of Hanger's amputation, he had no such drugs to relieve his pain. In fact, no anesthetics were available to him at all. And with the arteries ligated, the blood began to circulate again through his body, so he had just enough consciousness to be aware of every terrible step in the operation.

Dr. Robinson leaned over the leg and cut through the skin and bone using his crude knives and jagged saws. Small chips of bone lay soaked in the blood that pooled around the injury's center. Flies flocked to the blood, pestered around the operating table and landed upon the wound, where they stuck helpless in the mire. Even small pieces of dirt and cloth torn from Hanger's trousers during the collision with the cannonball somehow found a way into the open wound. Dr. Robinson worked carefully to extract all unwanted debris lest he stitch the wound with such infectious items still inside.

After severing the bone, Robinson used a file to smooth its surface. The slightest jagged protrusion of bone might aggravate the stump for an entire lifetime after it healed. Robinson tied the arteries closed while the assistants continued to hold the skin and tissue out of the way. Once the bone was filed and the arteries ligated, Robinson pulled the skin down on all sides to make a flap over the open wound. He formed the stump roundly in his hands like he would have shaped a snowball, then sealed the skin together with stitches placed about an inch apart. James Hanger had become the first amputee of the American Civil War.

In the pristine white sterilized rooms of hospitals today, amputation is a far less torturous process than it was when Dr. Robinson spent some 45 minutes detaching James Hanger's leg. Modern medical techniques now enable doctors to complete similar operations in a matter of minutes, and with little physical pain to the patient. Yet, no matter how great or weak the physical pain an individual is forced to endure, inevitably the greater difficulty occurs after the surgery, when the amputee first confronts the challenges of living with the loss of a limb.

In this sense, the mental trauma of amputation was no different for James Hanger back in 1861 than it is for any man, woman or child in today's fast-paced world. Limb loss knows no restrictions of race, religion, nationality or gender. *All amputees share in an initial sense of loss and despair.* Amputation can very easily push someone toward pessimism, apathy and depression, making it easy to give up hope of enjoying a life like the one before the amputation. In order not to sink into a slump of the sort easily spawned by limb loss, amputees must overcome the tendency toward hopelessness and make the most of the opportunities life does hand them. James Hanger recalled,

> *"I cannot look back upon those days in the hospital without a shudder. No one can know what such a loss means unless he has suffered a similar catastrophe. In the twinkling of an eye, life's fondest hopes seem dead. I was the prey of despair. What could the world hold for a maimed, crippled man! Today I am thankful for what seemed then to me nothing but a blunder of fate, but which was to prove instead a great opportunity."*

Similar emotions exist for amputees today. If Ed Hommer, Brian Frasure, and Dana Bowman had not understood the importance of making the most of adversity, they would never have accomplished what they have. For Ed, the towering

Mt. McKinley would be just another mountain from whose summit only the most headstrong and tough could gaze. To Brian, an eleven-second time in the 100-meter dash would be just another amazing feat for Olympians on TV. And for Dana, jumping from airplanes would be the adventuresome practice of those not burdened with his disability. Incredibly, like James Hanger, these men overcame their despair and seized opportunities. Some people simply will not be held down. In refusing to be held down himself, James Hanger opened the way for others like Ed, Brian and Dana to do the same.

A Productive Convalescence

After Hanger's amputation, the Union soldiers held him as a prisoner. A number of other Confederate volunteers were also taken prisoner and moved to various private homes until their releases could be negotiated. For two months James convalesced as a prisoner of the Union, during which time he was moved frequently. First he left the stable where he had incurred the injury, and moved into Philippi's small Methodist Episcopal Church, which had been converted into a hospital. At the makeshift hospital, the Union men gave James little time for recovery before moving him again to the home of Mr. and Mrs. William McClaskey, not far away. Mrs. McClaskey and her daughters tended to James and his injury. The McClaskey family supported the Confederacy, and was happy to help James in whatever way they could. But soon the Union forces took possession of their home, and moved James again, this time to a farm in the countryside known as Cherry Hill.

Although the war was young, Cherry Hill had already been established as a hospital for injured soldiers. The location would remain a hospital for most of the war, and it was there where James would acquire his first prosthetic limb. Technology at the time, however, was remedial and lacked functionality. His new limb was a heavy club of wood shaped like a peg. It attached to his stump crudely and with an awkward fit. The prosthesis shot straight from his stump to the ground with a rigid and cumbersome bulk that was no more graceful than a leg supporting a table. When he walked, James' steps would sound from yards away; with each stride one could hear the clomping caused by the awkward and unbalanced gait. The prosthesis he had been given epitomized the best technology available, but with every movement it wrought pain and strife. James survived with it as best he could, moving about to Camp Chase in Ohio, then on to Norfolk, Virginia, where he finally was exchanged as a prisoner in August of 1861.

From Norfolk, James returned home to Churchville. Only two months had passed since the eighteen-year-old had left home to enlist for the Confederacy, but so much had changed. In his mind he was still the vigorous and courageous chap who had set off through rain on horseback to meet his brothers in Philippi. But now, stumbling around on that peg leg, he was constantly burdened by discomfort, immobility and frustration.

Almost immediately, Hanger set to his room and insisted he not be disturbed. James' family perceived his reclusive behavior as an indication of the inner turmoil generated by the injury. What sorrow and grief an eighteen-year-old boy must feel to have lost a leg at such an early stage in life, they could not imagine; if only there was some way to help. But James made few requests. His one desire was to be left alone in his room upstairs, and the family obliged by giving him ample space and time. James' mother would bring meals upstairs, leave them outside his door, and an hour later she would return to find the plate cleaned. Occasionally, from downstairs, the family could hear James' door open and his clamorous clomping sounds pass across the hall. The sounds and the dinner plates gave assurance that James was still okay.

Now and then James made silly requests. He would ask for barrel staves and willow wood from the trees outside his home. Naturally the family assisted as they could. What crafts and pastimes a man can devise when grieving the loss of a limb, they could only guess. He was probably tormented by despair, and needed the wood to occupy his idle time, they supposed. After all, James had acquired something of a fancy for woodworking and engineering since returning from college. At night he would place buckets of shavings outside the door, and by morning they would be replaced with new wood for his carving games.

Three months passed. James and his family continued in the same distanced routine. The home functioned like James was not even around. When the family brought dinner upstairs or cleared away wood shavings, they did so as if these tasks were no different from any other on the household list of chores. The clomping sound of James stumbling above them melted into the continuum of sounds throughout the house, and converged among that din of noises whose individual parts one only notices on the moment they cease making noise. Communication between James and his family dropped to a minimum. They likely assumed he had sunk into a pit of depression, and they left him alone to cope with it himself.

Then one day something changed. An unfamiliar sound made a gentle trace over the stairs leading down from the second floor. No one could place it. The noise sounded like someone descending the stairwell, but there was no one up there except James, and he could hardly walk a yard without making a strident ruckus heard throughout the whole house. The strange sound approached closer still. Of all the people they expected to come down those stairs, the last one was James. But sure enough, there he was, eighteen-year-old James Hanger, ambling comfortably down the stairs with a stride so smooth it hardly seemed feasible. During his three-month isolation, James used barrel staves and willow wood to break a technological barrier that had stood for thousands of years. From the wood of his seemingly silly requests, he had made the world's first articulated double-joint prosthetic limb.

Fast Forward: An Amputee Skydiver Overcomes Adversity

If James Hanger's descent of the stairs in 1861 signaled a new era for prosthetic technology, then Dana Bowman's descent from the sky over a century later shows how far that new era has since progressed. A double amputee since 1994, Dana Bowman proves how Hanger Prosthetics & Orthotics can empower people with the capability to achieve their dreams. When James Hanger lost his leg in battle, he would not accept a rudimentary peg leg as his only replacement, so he fashioned a revolutionary leg that would endow him with the ability to function normally. When Dana Bowman lost his legs in a near fatal sky diving catastrophe, he too refused to be limited by a compromised lifestyle. Now he is back in the air, jumping from planes.

For Dana, the accident occurred on February 6, 1994, over the blistering skies of Yuma, Arizona. Dana belonged to the U.S. Army's elite Golden Knights skydiving team, and he was performing a routine training exercise called the Diamond

Track, in which he and a partner would use smoke to etch a diamond shape in the sky. Dana and his partner, Sgt. Jose Aguillon, had performed the routine together flawlessly almost 50 times. This was the second jump of the day, at around 10:00 a.m.

Dana Bowman lines up his parachute for landing. He proudly displays the American flag under his canopy for the crowd to see.

The Diamond Track jump began as usual. Both Dana and Sgt. Aguillon had a smoke canister attached to their ankles, and a cord that ran from the smoke bracket to their thighs. They would pull the cord when they hit the sky, then split in opposite directions, trying to stretch the maximum distance between them before converging again to complete the diamond at the bottom. All initial procedures went as planned. They jumped from the plane, initiated the smoke and split on different paths. But on the lower portion of the diamond, their bodies began to drift toward one another with unusually turbulent force. Dana could see the terror-stricken look of distress in Sgt. Aguillon's eyes. He ducked his head into his chest, but Aguillon's arm sliced down at 300 miles-per-hour, and severed both of Dana's legs like a sword passing through water. Aguillon, whose parachute failed to open, landed unconscious and near death in a tree. Dana hit ground in a parking lot.

Fortunately, an EMS team arrived quickly and airlifted the two men to the nearest hospital. Aguillon died of internal injuries almost immediately. Dana was unconscious, but doctors stopped the bleeding in his legs and sustained his breath. Two days later he awoke to find his partner and close friend dead, and his own legs amputated.

Without delay, Dana began his rehabilitation. Physical therapists drawing from past experience warned him that most double amputees never walk at all. Those words came as a challenge to a man who had already been through the most rigorous training courses in the world. Before the amputation, Dana graduated from the Armed Force's most difficult schools. He had been a Ranger, Sniper, Paratrooper and Special Forces Green Beret. In combat in Granada and Panama, he had earned several decorations. If a challenge existed that exacted the most physically grueling and mentally agonizing pain on man, then Dana Bowman had faced it and surpassed it. To be told he may never walk again was a fate he could not readily accept. The only hindrance was not his will, but the capacity for prosthetic technology to enable him to achieve all he desired. Fortunately, prosthetics would be the last thing to hold him down.

Doctors gave Dana six weeks to dispense with his crutches, but he tired of them in three days. At that point, Dana asked his doctors to remove the remaining infectious parts of his legs so he might be fit with artificial limbs. Dana imagined that he could use his prior mechanical expertise to fashion artificial limbs on his own. In fact, he did manage to construct two legs, using the same determination James Hanger used to construct his. Unlike Hanger, however, Dana's prosthetic legs were nothing revolutionary, and they soon caused him discomfort. When Dana realized his own prostheses were inferior to those he might find elsewhere, Dana sought the best prosthetic legs available, and Hanger Prosthetics & Orthotics, Inc., made just the ones. After converting to the "Hanger Legs," he enjoyed the functionality and comfort that no other imitation could offer. As early as November of that year, Dana re-enlisted with the Golden Knights and was once again jumping from planes, this time as the first double amputee ever to serve in the U.S. Army.

Five-hundred jumps later, a mandatory retirement policy forced Dana to retire from the Army after 16 years of dedicated service. His service to his country was exemplary, but even better was his positive contribution to improving the human spirit. Since retirement, Dana has toured the country giving inspirational speeches about the importance of struggling through adversity. He has motivated thousands by emphasizing that "disabled" does not mean "unable." Among his greatest wishes is the hope that his example and his speeches will make him a positive role model for both children and adults. Disabled people should be treated no differently than anyone else, he believes, because "it is the ability, and not the disability that counts."

Dana Bowman skydives across the United States and shares his incredible story of triumph.

With the advances in prosthetic limbs pioneered by Hanger Prosthetics & Orthotics, everyone who undergoes an amputation has the capability to overcome his or her disability. The distinction between the successful patient and the limited one is that some people never quit. Dana achieved his Bachelor's degree in Commercial Aviation at the University of North Dakota. In addition to sky diving, he is the first double amputee to earn a license to fly helicopters, seaplanes and hot air balloons. With his degree he aspires to fly for a commercial airline, as well.

Most of all, Dana Bowman keeps himself busy trying to make a positive contribution in the lives of others. His speeches address the threefold importance of hope, courage and determination when it comes to overcoming any challenge or obstacle. Over the last few years he has given over 450 speeches to colleges and universities, Boy Scouts, Veterans Hospitals, Rotary Clubs and the like. Although he realizes the importance of human will and perseverance, Dana also maintains an awareness of how physically dependent he is on prosthetic devices that function well enough to make his feats possible. Without Hanger Prosthetics & Orthotics, his capacity to overcome his loss might not even exist.

The Hanger Limb

The feats accomplished by all modern day amputees owe a large debt of gratitude to those innovators who made such spectacular accomplishments feasible. When, late in 1861, James Hanger walked confidently down his stairs on a new leg made of pliable wood, he became one of the preeminent forefathers of prosthetic technology; but others back then played significant parts as well.

Fifteen years before Hanger's invention, a New Yorker named Benjamin Franklin Palmer had claimed the first patent on an artificial limb. With big city connections in the Northeast, Palmer moved quickly in establishing a successful business and product. But while prosthetics became a "great and active branch of industry" during the war, scholar Oliver Wendell Holmes noted that artificial limbs only demanded "an occasional and exceptional want" before the 1860s. As a consequence, little attention was paid to improving Palmer's invention, until James Hanger became the war's first amputee and manufactured his own prosthesis. The Hanger leg vastly improved upon the Palmer limb; it truly opened up the possibility of a new era for prosthetics.

What made the Hanger leg so distinctive? First, James knew that comfort was a critical component of a good prosthetic device. Comfort depended upon alignment and fit. If the prosthetic device did not attach aligned at the appropriate angle or in the right direction, then it created a nuisance to wear. Even a slightly misaligned limb rendered it strenuous and painful to walk. Unfortunately, in the early years of prosthetics there were no technical gauges to provide accurate measurements of prosthetic leg lengths, and consequently, many prostheses at the time were made slightly too long or too short. This was particularly the case with lower body amputees, for whom errors in a prosthesis' length or size often caused a limp, back pain or stunted growth. Pain heightened even more when the cup that nested the stump of the residual limb chafed against the skin because it was too small, or when it shifted and blistered the skin because it was too large.

Functionality distinguished the new Hanger Limb in a second way. James knew that without functionality, a limb's comfort did not matter. Even if a peg leg could fit with complete ease, a rigid form would allow little chance for mobility. An unwieldy prosthesis had a limited range of motion, and without the ability to move freely, the prosthetic limb did not serve its purpose. The ideal goal of a prosthetic device, Hanger believed, was to restore the body to the way it functioned before the loss of limb. Comfort and function played a big part in that restoration, but they did not complete it.

Thirdly, Hanger recognized the undeniable importance of a prosthetic device's cosmetic appearance. No one wanted the stereotype of a "Peg Leg Pete." It was a sad fact that in our society, even injuries earned in war carried with them more insecurity and discomfort than they did heroic glory. The more realistic the substitute limb appeared, then, the greater chance the amputee had of blending in with a society of able bodied individuals. James knew there had to be a solution to minimize the discomfort of being ostracized as disabled. Until that time, though, there had not been a solution that met his approval.

Sequestered in his bedroom, James Hanger found a way to meld comfort, functionality and appearance. The Hanger

Limb was distinctive for its improvement upon the ways prior prostheses had failed. It was fashioned primarily with barrel staves and willow, two light yet durable woods. The decreased weight alleviated the burden that accompanied the use of heavier limbs, and the inclusion of a foot made it both sturdier and more realistic in appearance. Now, instead of hobbling around on an awkward leg, the Hanger Limb made walking fluid and less painful by adding two bending joints. Where before amputees stood out for the awkwardness of their disability, the new Hanger invention rivaled natural limbs as closely as possible. When someone saw him walking, James Hanger's substitute limb blended in with his real one.

Newspapers that saw his leg would report on it with extravagant praise. The editor of *The Vindicator* wrote of the leg, "It is one of the most complete legs we have ever seen." In response, the *Staunton Spectator* published a witty poem directed at *The Vindicator's* editor:

The "most complete" limb he ever did see was Hanger's wooden L.E.G.

Aside from the attempt at jest, the *Spectator* also offered praise about Hanger's work:

> *"Mr. Hanger, being possessed of good mechanical ingenuity, and too patriotic to be dependent upon the Yankees for an artificial leg, invented by his own genius, and manufactured by his own skill, an artificial leg, by which he is enabled to walk with ease."*

While the articles about Hanger's injury and recovery did not furnish expansive details, they attest to the attention given Hanger's new prosthesis.

Newspapers were not the only ones to notice the artificial limb. Not long after James descended the stairs flaunting his new invention, other amputees noticed its amazing advantages. They approached him hoping that he might fashion them similar prosthetic devices. Hanger in turn made every effort to accommodate the needs of fellow amputees. Although the war was young, action had intensified since the first skirmish between Confederate and Union soldiers at Philippi, and the need for good prosthetic devices was more immediate than ever before. Amputations accounted for an alarming three-fourths of all battlefield operations. Hanger's timing was perfect, and his good will was even better.

He relocated to Richmond, Virginia after his convalescence, and began by fitting a few other injured veterans with prostheses. With a constant mind for improvement, Hanger quickly acquired a reputation as one of the South's best and most innovative manufacturers of prosthetic devices. Unlike many other products, the Hanger Limb served as its own endorsement; one needed only see the leg to realize its obvious advantages.

As Hanger's work progressed and improved, it drew the attention of surgeon William Carrington, corresponding secretary of the Association for the Relief of Maimed Soldiers. In a letter responding to Dr. Carrington's inquiry, Hanger explained the remarkable new improvements he had made with his prosthetic leg:

> *"The principle is the same as that of the Palmer leg. With the following improvements:*
>
> *1st—The hinge of the knee is placed back 1/2 an inch (more or less) in the rear of the centre of the leg, which prevents it from flexing, while the*

weight is upon it, without it being bent backwards further than the natural limb, and which renders it much easier to the wearer.

2nd—The springs are made of caoutchouc, operating by compression which renders them superior to those operating by elongation, because they cannot be broken, and because they do not become weaker by long and continued use; superior to the metallic springs because the weather has no effect on them and are not subject to rust and hence the operation of the springs is the same at all times. By the peculiar arrangement of the spring and lever which passes through it, the spring can be made stronger or weaker at the pleasure of the wearer.

3rd—The bolts of the joints pass through brass boxes or thimbles, instead of the wood, rendering little or no wear by friction, hence avoiding the necessity of busking or of its becoming loose by long use, and requires but little oiling.

The heel cord, made of raw hide, extends from the heel up above the knee joint, and is attached directly over the knee bolt, hence the knee will not flex when the weight is brought forward on the toes. The advantage of its being attached above the knee instead of below, is, that when the knee is flexed in the act of walking, the cord slackens, thus permitting the toes to be raised by the action of the ankle spring and to pass over an obstruction. The stuffed pad or sole of the foot is detached from the foot and is designed to be placed in the boot or shoe first as an inside sole, so that the boot can be drawn on or off easily.

The wood of which the leg is made is very light and tough, the irons are securely fastened by rivets; the whole leg is enveloped with raw hide which strengthens the wood much more than leather or any other material and then painted and varnished. Weighs 4 lbs. 14 1/2 oz."

Excerpt From a Letter from James E. Hanger to Dr. William Carrington, February 16, 1864.

At the time of the letter, Hanger had already formed a company for his enterprise of providing prostheses. More immediately following his injury, though, no standardized marketplace for prosthetic devices even existed. Before any business venture began, Hanger first made limbs on good will. He recalled of those first months after his recovery:

"I started out to overcome the handicap of the loss of a leg — to overcome it in the best possible way — and that has been the one and only goal I have striven to reach. In a word, I did not say 'Will this limb sell?' and then having decided that it would sell, try to create for it a market. I asked myself 'Will this best take the place of what misfortune has destroyed?'"

Having lost a limb himself, Hanger knew the perils of amputation too well to exploit the use of his prosthetic device. If his fellow amputees had inferior prostheses, then he strove to replace them with devices of higher quality. Truly, James Hanger's intentions were humanitarian and philanthropic. The day came, though, when his prostheses became increasingly popular and the only natural choice was to form a business that enabled him to meet the needs of more of his disabled countrymen.

The Birth of an Enterprise

The Civil War Era was a perfect time for the birth of a new business. As the war wrought an unprecedented legacy of crippled and amputated men, it opened the opportunity for an entire industry devoted to prosthetics. If "War unmakes legs," wrote Oliver Wendell Holmes, then "human skill must supply their places." James Hanger had the skill to do so, and by making a prosthetic limb that improved upon all others available, he slipped into the forefront of those opportunists in life who confront a misfortune and make of it the most they can. He lived the American Dream, and soon, the J.E. Hanger Company thrived in Richmond.

The social climate in America at the time involved mid-century ideals that amputees should be entitled to social provisions like health care and welfare. In response, the government began pension plans for disabled veterans, in many cases entitling veterans to incremental payments of social welfare depending upon the anatomical location and extent of their disability. A veteran who had lost a hand, for instance, received more money than one who had lost only his fingers. Virginia passed "an act to provide artificial limbs for the citizens of the Commonwealth who lost their limbs in the late war." The state chose a company that could "combine in the highest degree utility and economy" to furnish those limbs. As the best prosthetic company around, the Commonwealth of Virginia chose the J.E. Hanger Company as the one to manufacture artificial limbs for wounded Confederate veterans.

Immediately, business flourished. Workloads increased, and the commission earned from the Commonwealth helped the J.E. Hanger Company take on more business without compromising its quality of service. Given all its success, it would have been easy to forget the humanitarian and service-oriented principles on which the company was founded. But from the outset, Hanger ensured these values were always a priority. As he reflected later in life,

> *"There is sound logic in our determination not to extend our activities beyond our capacity. If we have learned no other lesson, we are fully convinced of the wisdom of the policy we have followed all these years, never to allow our output to grow faster than our standards of quality and individual attention will allow."*

While he remained cautious about growing faster than the company's capabilities, James Hanger never once stood idle in the quest to make better prosthetic devices. His products always shimmered on the cutting edge of technology. Yet, his innovative spirit did not end with the ingenuity of his prosthetic creations. Hanger also brought a new caliber of service, and a new type of business to the market. In this regard, the humanitarian intentions of all his endeavors cannot be given enough reward. His chief interest always remained to provide a better lifestyle for those members of what he deemed the world's great "brotherhood" of amputees. As a businessman, too, he showed keen judgement as only a true opportunist could. "I will cheerfully submit to all inconveniences and deprivations," he once wrote, "provided I can do it with consistency to pecuniary interest, for the welfare of the country is always as ever has been the principle thought of my mind." With a genuine concern for social welfare, and a poignant sense for business, James Hanger was able to build a prosperous company without jeopardizing his goal to provide amputees with sound and highly individualized care.

Soon the company grew bigger still. In 1871, Hanger patented his substitute limb and moved his office from the corner of a carpenter's shop in Richmond back to his hometown of Churchville. His company was by then a widely recognized and highly acclaimed name in the prosthetics industry. The stream of injured veterans returning from the war only helped boost its reputation even more. After all, most Confederate veterans turned to the J.E. Hanger Company for their needs because their care was provided for by the Virginia legislature.

With a solid foundation underneath him from a business perspective, James availed himself of the opportunity to pursue his personal life. In 1873 he married a kind and maternal woman named Nora McCarthy, who would bear six sons and two daughters for their family. James reared all his children to practice the same strong morals he already possessed. With maturity, they would come to carry on the family business into the century that ensued.

Before handing over his business, though, James continued the forward path of excellence on his own. He was no longer the young and inexperienced boy he had been when he left for the war. Since then he had become every bit a man, and with adulthood he had grown into a charming and attractive gentleman. Those who knew him best held him dear for his quick wit and wry sense of humor. Perhaps more than all else, James Hanger had an unquenchable thirst for life. The optimism and positive outlook he brought to the world spread like an epidemic blessing among those around him. James never wallowed indoors or complained about his unlucky fate. Instead, he took up golf, and he frequently found beauty in the natural wonders of the world, truly refusing to allow his injury to hold him back.

Given the prosthetic technologies he pioneered, it was easier for him and other amputees to make the most of the world. The greatest difficulty was mental, not physical. "I know your feelings and your problems," Hanger told amputees, "But the world is just as beautiful as of old. The flowers and the trees and the sunshine are just as precious as ever. Nor has opportunity fled. Science and invention have done, and are doing, more to cancel your misfortune than can possibly be done for any other serious handicap in life."

Hanger's words were true. In 1883 he moved the company to Washington, D.C., and shortly opened branches in Atlanta, then St. Louis, then Pittsburgh, then Philadelphia and Baltimore. With innovations constantly developed, and new patents made frequently, the J.E. Hanger Company was poised to provide amputees the newest and best prosthetic equipment, not only in the South, but all over the nation.

Dima Sitnik lost both legs in 1993 in a train accident near Minsk, Belarus. He now lives in the United States and plays golf wearing prosthetic legs. Dima did not play golf prior to the accident.

The national care on which Hanger founded his company has long since evolved into a worldwide effort to improve the lives of amputees. Hanger Prosthetics & Orthotics, Inc. now helps people all over the world overcome the challenges of living with the loss of a limb. In 1999, Hanger helped a team of runners from the Achilles Track Club in Hanoi to participate in the New York City Marathon by donating the artificial limbs they needed to compete. In 1994, Hanger gave three months of clinical care to help fit a poor disabled boy from Minsk, Belarus with two artificial legs.

The stories are endless, and merely to list them all would not accurately depict the magnitude of emotion and triumph each one entails. The reason no list can depict these stories fully is because each one involves the human heart, body and spirit. The pain that amputees suffer from having lost a limb cannot be qualified by description anymore than words can convey the joy that greets amputees when their loss is replaced with a functional prosthesis. Yet, a list of the people that Hanger has helped might read like a list of heralded soldiers on a national memorial. The difference would be size;

Hanger's list would include veterans, children, women and laymen alike. Despite their nationality, economic status, or any other characteristic by which people can be divided, each of Hanger's patients is more than just another customer. They are heroes.

Brian Frasure, below-knee amputee, competes in the men's T-44 200 meter sprint in the 2000 Paralympic Games in Sydney, Australia.

Fast Forward: A World Class Sprinter With Only One Leg

The heroism of one Hanger patient, Brian Frasure, had its birth in a tragedy that occurred when Brian was a sophomore track star at North Carolina State University. One night, while studying inside his dorm room, Brian heard the sound of a freight train approaching outside. He and his friends were adventuresome youngsters, and they had a game whereby they ran alongside passing trains and tried to jump on the cars for an adrenaline rush. Most often the trains would slow down as they passed through the area, so the dangers seemed relatively minor. But that night, as he and some buddies hurried outside to catch the action, the train moved swiftly. Brian was not perturbed. He had strong legs, and he sprinted parallel to the tracks waiting for an opportune moment to make the leap and grasp hold of a ladder on one of the moving cars. When his moment arrived, he leaped for the ladder but tripped. Brian tumbled forward and his feet fell under the passing cars; two sets of wheels ran them over.

A few hours later, Brian lay in a hospital bed with his left leg amputated slightly below the knee. As a runner, nothing could be worse than losing a leg he depended upon so much. He wished he were dead rather than have no leg; there seemed nothing to be done.

Brian took the semester off from school, and when he returned he still had not replaced the missing limb with an artificial substitute. Classmates and strangers stared at him as he hobbled around campus on his crutches. It must have been strange to see a talented track star so disabled, but it must have been stranger still for Brian to adjust to a handicapped lifestyle after having always been so quick and adroit.

Soon he would have that speed and deftness back, when he decided to have Hanger Prosthetics & Orthotics fit him with a prosthetic leg. The Hanger leg, made of carbon fiber and attached below his knee, gave Brian more capabilities than he ever imagined a prosthetic device could offer. Rather than quit running, Brian began training again. The speed he had before the injury did not take long to recover; and, remarkably, the prosthetic leg did not slow him down.

At 27, Brian Frasure became one of the fastest men alive. He set the below-the-knee amputee world record in the 100-meter dash, posting a time of 11.33 seconds at an intense competition in Sydney, Australia in 1999. During the race, the rain and slick track made conditions slower than usual. In the 2000 Paralympic Games, he earned silver medals in both the 100- and 200-meter sprint. Now he aims one day to become the first amputee ever to score a 100-meter sprint time under eleven seconds.

Regardless of Brian's future excellence on the track, he has already been a positive role model off it. Since his injury, Brian has finished his education at N.C. State by following in the footsteps of James Hanger. Both men studied engineering. Both men also turned their lives in similar directions after their amputation. Brian used his bachelor's degree from N.C. State to further his education at Northwestern University, where he successfully completed a specialized prosthetic education program. Given all that Hanger did to change Brian's life, he found it only natural to give something back in return. Now he counsels Hanger's amputee patients about the mental, physical and emotional difficulties of adjusting to their new lives. He

Amputee athlete, Brian Frasure, uses a specially designed prosthesis to allow him to compete in track meets throughout the world.

enjoys demonstrating the ease with which he walks, and when he is around new amputees, Brian flaunts his own confidence of stride—not to remind them of their disabilities, but to show them the possibilities that await them through Hanger's superior limbs.

While Brian Frasure epitomizes the injured athlete who overcame adversity to be a champion, there are countless stories of people whose lifestyles have much more modest goals. Hanger Prosthetics & Orthotics does not, after all, exclusively aid those whose natural talents are extraordinary. More often the company helps ordinary people beset by misfortune recover their ability to perform everyday tasks and take part in recreational activities. The company helps youngster Keaton Ramsey learn to ride his bicycle; it helps David Kirkwood train to fly airplanes; it helps Phyllis Frohlich continue to sew and cook as well as change her grandchild's diapers. Again, a list does not do justice to the triumphant capabilities Hanger has restored. Most importantly, remember this: Hanger does not make dreams come true; Hanger gives people the physical ability to make dreams come true on their own.

Ethan Wright, born without his right arm (below-elbow), utilizes an activity-specific prothesis to enable him to play the violin.

Hanger's Enterprise Grows

As his life progressed, James Hanger saw his dreams come true in the form of his growing business. The J.E. Hanger Company incorporated in 1906, when James was 63. He had started out on a personal crusade to assist a few comrades-in-arms, and in a single lifetime he had built a company with successful facilities all over the country. Soon, James retired from an active business role and took time to enjoy the recreational facets of life. He played more golf, and he enjoyed the company of his friends in the Church. James was an elder in the Presbyterian Church of Georgetown, D.C. from April 1898 to April 1908, and then again from 1911 until his death in 1919. Peers delighted in his kind nature, and commended him for his sincerity and loyalty, particularly to his cause. But almost a decade after the turn of the century, it was time to integrate his children into the company.

With the First World War beginning in Europe, the timing was perfect. As he had done for Civil War veterans at home, James found it also important to help wounded Allies abroad. He sent some of his older children to Europe, where they would control the international branches of the business. Already the company had a thriving practice throughout the eastern half of the United States, and a move to London and Paris made sense because the war had created a great need for prosthetic services among European countries. James sent his son Hoover to manage the Paris factory, and his son Hugh went to manage in London. Another one of his sons, Bert, visited Italy, where he examined the possibility of building another facility.

The move to Europe was not purely spontaneous; it came by invitation. The Red Cross sought out the Hanger Company and gave them large contracts to make limbs for the wounded soldiers in Paris. Much like the commission earned from the U.S. government during the American Civil War, the British government also hired the Hanger Company to fashion limbs for wounded veterans in London. The opportunity to help more people all over the world could not be missed. The Hanger Company even undertook efforts to furnish limbs for South American mining engineers, Chinese missionaries, and

Hawaiian and Philippine civilians. Although James had essentially retired, he remained active as president, and kept an advisory capacity that helped ensure the Hanger name was well represented overseas.

In Europe, the Hanger children soon discovered that the European countries were far behind the United States in prosthetic technology. James attributed the discrepancy to the far greater demand for prosthetic assistance in the United States over the last fifty years. In particular, the period of industrialization surrounding the American Civil War made the need for prosthetic limbs more pressing than previously. Accidental on-the-job injuries were more common than before, and the War wrought its own group of amputees. America's pressing need spawned new prosthetic advances that were not prevalent in Europe until the Hanger Company moved there during the First World War.

When the Hanger Company expanded to Europe, it sought not only to provide quality artificial limbs for wounded veterans, but to teach Europeans some of the Company's basic principles about prosthetics. Namely, the Company reinforced its belief that there is no such thing as making quality prosthetics by wholesale. Notwithstanding the incredible demand, the Hanger Company continued to emphasize personalized care. To Hanger, artificial limbs could not be made like shoes that come in certain sizes that are "tried-on" by various amputees. Rather, every patient must be measured individually to ensure the utmost accuracy in fit. *Then*, from the measurements, a limb can be designed to meet the exact specifications of every amputee. While the wartime demand made it difficult to maintain these practices, the Hanger Company remained faithful to its most valuable tenets of customer service and individualized attention.

Maintaining a standard of high quality care in the Company's European facilities proved more difficult from a practical standpoint than it ever was from an ideological one. Measurements for the limbs were taken locally from patients in Europe, but crude versions of the limbs were first manufactured in the United States. The crude limbs would then be sent overseas, where prosthetists in the London and Paris branches would trim and sculpt them to suit each individual case. Shipping crudely fabricated limbs across the ocean may seem like an exorbitant inconvenience, but to the J.E. Hanger Company, it was the only way to assure customers that the prostheses they received were made from the best materials available on the planet.

Oddly enough, the wood that was used to make the limbs was indigenous to England. Years ago, however, great portions of the English Willow had been transported to America and planted along the James River, among other waterways. By the time of the first World War, the willow tree grew in America with such abundance that it actually made more sense to ship it from the United States than to use the remaining supply found in England. Naturally, a portion of the wood for the limbs came directly from England, but the greater majority made the trip overseas. The organization behind this process, and the successful implementation of what would seemingly have been an inefficient endeavor, exemplifies the Hanger Company's size and skill during the first decade after the century's turn.

Back stateside, the J.E. Hanger Company faced a barrage of competitors. To James, they did not pose much of a concern. He knew they did not operate with the same thoroughness and quality as his own company. "From almost the first days that the Hanger Artificial Limb was placed on the market there have been imitators and competitors," Hanger reflected. The reason the Hanger Company has stayed on top is its unparalleled product and care. As Hanger explained:

> *"It has worked simply this way: The first few men for whom we made limbs must have felt that we supplied their wants in the best way, for they sent others to us, until a few hundred had come; and they in turn sent others until we had many hundreds of customers, and these hundreds soon grew to thousands. All of which goes to prove the old saying that if you make anything better than it has been made before, though you live in a wilderness, the world will make a beaten path to your door."*

James' explanation for the company's success is especially accurate given how little emphasis the company placed on advertising. James Hanger always believed that the most powerful advertisements came from first hand encounters with the product itself. So long as those who wore his limbs had reason to praise them, he believed, then the Hanger name would continue to hold respect and recognition. Accordingly, unlike many of his northern competitors, Hanger expended minimal funds on advertising and devoted the majority of the company's money to improving its products. As he viewed the situation, advertisements sought to reach people in large masses. He, on the other hand, sought to personalize relationships with individual people, one at a time.

One relationship Hanger made serves as an ideal example of how he envisioned the Hanger name should be promoted. On the way to work every morning, Hanger used to see an elderly man begging for change on a street corner near the Capital building in Washington, D.C. The man was obviously poor, and disabled, too. Both his legs had been amputated above the knee. Each day people would pass him by without regard. At the end of the working day, Hanger would return on the same route to see the old man there in the identical position, his outstretched hat only graced with the addition of a few petty coins. As a man of genuine philanthropy, James Hanger was unable to let this fellow amputee go without care. Despite the stigma he knew might come from showing fondness to a minority at that time in the South's history, it made little difference to James that the beggar was a man of color. What James saw was a man in need of two legs. He took the man in to his shop and fit him, free of charge, with two of the company's newest and most functional prosthetic limbs. From James' perspective, there could be no better advertisement for his company than a person whose life has improved for the better thanks to Hanger Limbs. Eventually, the man and James became close friends, and James hired him to work in his Washington laboratory. It was not long before the old man mastered his new legs and learned to walk and move about with the vivacity of a man half his age. The new limbs invigorated his life—a fact that delighted Hanger every time he would walk up stairs or climb a ladder. To James, whose life was nearing its end, this patient and eventual friend symbolized the individual care he had sought to provide for all amputees over the world.

Today, Hanger Prosthetics & Orthotics continues to let the endorsements of its successful patients promote the company name. In the modern prosthetic industry, the Hanger name already draws immediate associations of innovation, excellence, and honest, individualized care. The unconsciously made endorsements found in the company's myriad success stories reinforce the positive associations the Hanger name has already earned.

Ed Hommer, double below-knee amputee, takes a break during his incredible journey to Mt. McKinley's peak.

Fast Forward: Hanger Patient Tops Mountains?

Another of the company's crowning success stories is that of Ed Hommer, bi-lateral amputee from Duluth, Minnesota. In 1981, Ed was a commercial pilot in a small Alaskan town named Talkeetna. His days consisted primarily of flying climbers to base camp on the lower portion of Mt. McKinley. The route was simple, and although the mountain often held turbulent weather systems, he had made the routine safely too many times to recount. One day in December, Ed took three friends with him in a four-seat airplane to have a scenic view of the mountain. He followed the same routine as usual, but that day especially blustery weather tormented the skies. Winter winds and heavy snow threw the tiny aircraft beyond his control. Vision blurred with whiteness, and the shaking plane drew closer to the mountain until, too close, it crashed into a wall of ice and snow.

The four men evacuated the plane, but found nowhere to go. They had survived the crash with a miracle, but now they had to wait in hope that a team of rescuers would come save them. None of the men could be sure a team would even come. The group's radio had been destroyed with the accident, and they had no other means to communicate with people in Talkeetna. Even worse, their food supply had disappeared with the wreck. Without drink or shelter, Ed Hommer and his friends' hope for survival looked grim.

Over the next five days, the mountain took two of the four stranded men. Temperatures sunk to 30 degrees below zero, and winds blew at over 100 miles per hour. Ed recalls a breaking point when he had to decide whether to hang on long enough to live, or instead give up and die. Frozen, and near death already, Ed persevered. Without shelter, there was little he could do but cling stubbornly to this determined will to survive. The cold gnawed at his legs, and by the time he and his surviving partner were rescued, he had staved off death, but the bitter clench of frostbite had claimed his legs.

Life without legs does not come easily for anyone, but for someone as active as Ed Hommer, it came as complete devastation. He was fit with an inadequate pair of limbs that demanded he use two canes just to walk. The bicycling, hiking and running that he did before the injury were now mere dreams hindered by his two shoddy limbs and the canes he used for balance. After being so determined to survive while stuck on the mountain, he pulled through only to find his life become a mere fraction of the fully functional life he remained so insistent to save.

Five years after the plane accident, in his hometown of Duluth, Ed visited a Hanger prosthetist. When the prosthetist promised to have Ed resume his active lifestyle, the despair that had followed Ed since the crash faded away, replaced by hope and determination. After taking precise measurements and paying close personal attention to his needs, the Hanger prosthetist fit Ed with the latest in prosthetic limb advancements. The new legs were made with custom-shaped flexible sockets designed to contour and intimately fit the bones and muscles of the residual limb. Not only would they let Ed put down his canes, but they would enable him to bike over sixty miles a day, and even continue to fly for a commercial airline.

Never in his life did Ed Hommer dream such feats were possible after sustaining an injury like his. Ed not only proved to himself that such feats were possible, he proved to the world that prosthetic limbs made a lot more possible still. In 1999, Ed returned to Alaska's Mt. McKinley, this time to face the mountain that had claimed both his legs and the lives of two close friends. Ed had a mission not only to confront the mountain and make peace with it, but also to become the world's first double-amputee to reach the summit. "The mountain took my legs," Ed likes to say, "but it didn't take my spirit."

Historically, Mt. McKinley is itself a spiritual place. Native Americans in the area call it "Denali," meaning "high one." The description fits nicely, for McKinley has the highest and coldest peak on the North American continent. At 20,320 feet, it towers over the wilderness and peaks among the clouds. For anyone to reach the top is incredible, but for a man with two prosthetic legs to do it is downright amazing. In 1998, Hommer had tried for a complete ascent of the mountain, but tempestuous weather conditions deterred his attempt. Two of the men in his expedition quit when the weather turned nasty, but Ed and a friend named Kelley Raymond remained on the mountain. They waited for the weather to clear, hiking whenever they could, but it was not to be. Hommer and Raymond turned back. They would have to wait another year.

By the time the next year arrived, Ed Hommer and climbing partner Kelley Raymond were ready again. On May 19, they left from Mt. McKinley's base camp eager to finish what they started. This time the weather conditions were much more favorable. In only a week, the two men reached the high camp at 17,200 feet. From there they would launch their final ascent to the summit. First they had to wait for the weather to improve. Not long before their expedition began, a group of climbers from Britain had been stranded at the high camp and rescued by emergency helicopters. At that altitude, hiking toward the summit posed extreme dangers. Ed's plane crash had taken place at 9,000 feet, and it had been treacherous there; at twice the altitude, the winds and cold were even fiercer. Take into account the oxygen shortage and avalanche risks, and you can see how easy it might be to retreat. Nevertheless, Ed and

Kelley fought through the harsh winds, thick snows and thin air to accomplish what they set out to achieve. On June third, Ed Hommer planted a flag into the snow and gazed out over the earth below. He had reached the summit.

After his successful conquest over Mt. McKinley, Ed set larger goals. In March of 2000, he went to Nepal with an American/Canadian expedition. The Himalayan mountain range that runs a latitudinal course across Nepal has eight of the top 14 highest mountains in the world. Ed and his expedition aspired to climb the Singu Chuli Peak, which has a 22,000 foot summit in the Anapuruna region of the Himalayas.

The expedition began well; the thrills and adventures of Nepalese culture fascinated the team. They began in Katmandu and hired local porters to lead them on their way up the mountain. Torrential rains made their trek to the base camp slow going. On the way in, some of the porters went on strike, which later forced the expedition to take a different route up the mountain. The new route was heavily exposed to wind and snow. Already the team had incurred several encounters with avalanches, some of which they barely eluded. Despite their good fortune with safety and health, however, the new route was to be too dangerous and time-consuming to attempt. It would have required them to take a route no climber had taken in the last 30 years. Ed was adept and capable of reaching the peak, but this new course was not advisable. Sadly, then, the ascent of Singu Chuli Peak was destined to the same fate as Hommer's first attempt on Mt. McKinley. It was not to be.

Not all ended in disappointment, though, because Hommer still managed to reach the summit of a nearby peak named Tharpu Chuli, with an elevation of 18,700 feet. In whole, he viewed the expedition as a success, even if he could not reach his intended summit. Just by trying and by enduring the difficulties, Ed proved a lot about the capabilities of amputees who wear Hanger prostheses. He reflects:

> *"I had the opportunity to speak with people from all over the world about prosthetic limbs and the advancements that have been made in the capable human spirit that each of us possess. Not to merely endure, but to excel with the great promise that life still holds against what may seem long odds at times. We should all remember in our lives that courage is not always marked by a roar, but more often by quietly saying at day's end, I will try again tomorrow."*

Ed's determination and perseverance are an inspiration to most anyone who hears his story. Yet, the story of his Himalayan journey does not end with his ascent of Tharpu Chuli.

While visiting Nepal, Ed discovered to his disappointment that the country lacks the resources to provide amputees with sound prosthetic devices. After speaking with both surgeons and amputees, he realized how easily the situation could be remedied. Ed's next mission is to bring modern prosthetic technology and equipment to Nepal. "With assistance and a solid team," he says, "We will change this. There is no reason not to. It can be done."

Ed plans a return to Nepal. He will take on his new mission then, and fit in a climb while he is at it— up a peak called Mt. Everest.

Ed Hommer died September 23, 2002, while training on Mt. Rainier in Washington State.

The Hanger Orthopedic Group: James Hanger's Legacy

One sign of a true winner is the ability to set high goals, then continually strive to achieve them. Ed Hommer represented the Hanger name so well because his persistence and determination resemble those same qualities on which James Hanger sought to build and improve his company. Even at the age of 72, James Hanger still sought innovation at every turn.

In 1915, James spent a year touring Europe. The Great War (WWI) brought forth a new need for prosthetics, and from it had come new possibilities in limb structure and fabrication. Though he was old and retired, he still made the journey to research those advances that would keep him on the brink of new inventions. Hanger always carried with him the goal of perpetual innovation.

While touring Europe, the British Government officially commended Hanger for his lifetime of service to amputees all over the world. At that point, the company was in the good hands of his children, and no technologies or innovations bypassed them. James had worked hard to ensure that the personalized service of the J.E. Hanger Company would never be compromised for wholesale output or dishonest prosperity. As he neared his end, after a life spent giving every part of his existence to making better lives for amputees, James Hanger reflected on success.

> *"I wonder after all if success should be judged entirely from a money standpoint. Is the mere making of money comparable to the gratification of helping thousands in the best possible way you can help a man, and that is to help him help himself? I don't think it is, and I am content."*

Indeed, James Hanger deserved to feel content. He had gained great wealth in his lifetime, but he had never placed profit in front of the need to help people help themselves.

Less than four years after returning stateside, Mr. Hanger died in Washington, D.C., on June 9, 1919. His wife Nora had died in April of that same year, and both were survived by all eight of their children. James left more behind than a strong family of offspring. In a single lifetime he had pioneered an entirely new market for prosthetic limbs. More remarkably, he had done it with the sole intent to provide amputees with the best, most efficient prosthetic limbs available. The limb he made after his own amputation advanced a long-standing trend of poor prosthetic devices by proving to be more functional, more comfortable and more attractive than anything else to precede it. By the time of his death, his innovations spoke for themselves.

Along with acquiring new patents on improved versions of his prosthetic limbs and braces, he imagined and perfected several other inventions as well. Among his inventions were a shampoo bowl and chair, a special bed to sleep outdoors, a Venetian blind, a water turbine and a horseless carriage. The horseless carriage operated as a toy, and he presented it to his youngest children for their amusement long before the invention of the first automobile. Most remembered, of course, are his advancements in the field of prosthetics. Hanger also holds a patent for a planograph lathe, which he used to assist in the manufacturing of his famous limbs. After what James Hanger did for the world, prosthetic limbs were no longer *just* prosthetic limbs; they were "Hanger Limbs," and that distinction made all the difference.

Almost a century after James Hanger's death, his ideals still drive the growing company he began. Today, the prosthetics and orthotics division of Hanger Orthopedic Group, Inc. is the world's largest provider of orthotic and prosthetic services and products. The Hanger name is to prosthetics and orthotics what Kleenex is to tissue, or what Xerox is to photocopies. While Hanger's original principles still drive the company, since his death, the company has gradually expanded in accordance with the needs of its times.

After World War I, the rehabilitation process for amputees earned more attention than it had in the past. Consumer groups formed to provide support for amputees and to discuss potential improvements in prosthetic equipment. In 1921, the U.S. Congress created the Veterans Administration, which operated hospitals and provided vocational rehabilitation for the disabled. The Hanger Company remained involved. Little advancements were made, however, until World War II. With the Second World War the Veterans Administration expanded, and accompanying it came technologies that had never before existed. Rather than wood, plastic became a popular material for artificial limbs. An emphasis swung from restoring basic functionality, to returning amputees to active and productive lifestyles. Again, the Hanger Company remained at the forefront of advancements in this direction.

Soon there arrived a boom period in the prosthetic industry. In response to the 1930s, when the Depression hit hard on the American home front, the Federal Government passed legislation to assist in the rehabilitation of the handicapped. Schools later began offering programs to train prosthetists and physical therapists. All along, the Hanger Company had advocated the need to educate and train people in the field of prosthetics. Once accredited schools started doing so, the advancements in the prosthetics industry came more quickly than before. From this high period came a new attention to orthotics as well as prosthetics.

Whereas prosthetics is a field that deals with artificial limbs, orthotics is a field that deals with braces and supports. Both are involved in the custom designing, fabrication and fitting of serviceable devices for the injured and impaired. When spoken of today, prosthetics and orthotics are almost

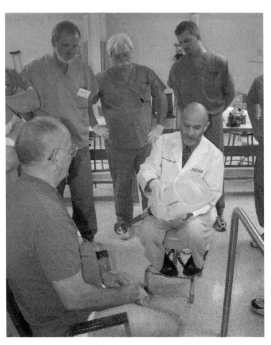

Each month, Hanger practitioners attend an educational training course on the unique design and fitting techniques of the patented Hanger ComfortFlex™ Socket System.

always paired together. The Hanger Orthopedic Group, Inc. is no longer just a provider of prosthetic limbs. Orthotics and prosthetics share equally as important roles in the company's services. When it comes to quality patient care, Hanger Prosthetics & Orthotics, Inc., is unparalleled in the industry.

Hanger Prosthetics & Orthotics operates nearly 600 patient care facilities nationwide, including an employee base of approximately 900 certified practitioners. Hanger's provider network allows almost 400 managed care organizations to

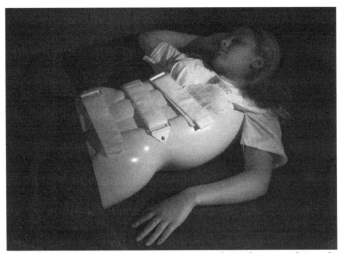

The Charleston Bending Brace is a noctunal (nightime only) orthosis designed to be effective in managing scoliosis.

contract for O & P services with member practitioners at independent patient care centers. With national health care programs and referral systems that point patients toward Hanger, anyone who stands to benefit from prosthetics or orthotics can be promised high quality and personalized care.

It is not easy to perceive the magnitude of the Hanger Orthopedic Group's growth since the death of its founding father. In July of 1999, Hanger acquired NovaCare Orthotics & Prosthetics Division in the largest acquisition in Hanger's history. The acquisition enabled Hanger Orthopedic Group, Inc. to earn a market share of roughly one-fourth of the O & P market. In a market of such massive size, Hanger's one-fourth share gives the Company the chance to change thousands of lives every day.

Nevertheless, the merger of the nation's two largest prosthetic and orthotic companies has not changed the industry's landscape as much as it might seem. The acquisition did not so much as expand the industry, as unify it by consolidating the network of existing practices.

It is amazing that even today, the corporate goals of the Hanger Orthopedic Group, Inc. emphasize service over profit. The company's stated mission is as follows:

> *"To be the best in providing the most advanced orthotic and prosthetic services available, and provide orthotic and prosthetic services in a timely and professional manner, in a pleasant atmosphere, and at a reasonable cost to our patients, and continually strive to improve our services and facilities, while maintaining a rewarding atmosphere for our associates and investors."*

Thanks to the company's speed of growth and emphasis on the quality of local practices, most would agree that Hanger Orthopedic Group, Inc. has upheld, and will continue to uphold its mission.

Fortune magazine, September 1999 issue, chose Hanger Orthopedic Group, Inc., as one of the fastest growing companies in America. Of the thousands of companies in the country, Hanger ranked 74th in the *Fortune* assessment. The magazine's Internet publication explains Hanger's position simply: "Hanger dominates the market for specialty orthotic and prosthetic services." The statement is appropriate. Remarkably, though, the company's growth and financial success have not compromised its original principles.

Maintaining strong principles and unmatched quality in a cutthroat global marketplace can be a difficult task. This task is even more trying given the responsibilities that have arisen in response to the success Hanger Orthopedic Group, Inc. has earned since its genesis following the Civil War. The responsibility comes in many forms. As the oldest prosthetics and orthotics company in the nation, for instance, Hanger has a duty to uphold the standard of excellence it first set under its founder. Presently, the Company fulfills its responsibilities of leadership in multiple ways; its formula for success, however, has remained undeviating. In order to provide top quality customer service, Hanger continues to pride itself on education, charity and innovation.

The Hanger Group has remained at the top of its industry through well-orchestrated training efforts to improve customer service. Approximately 700 of Hanger's practitioners are accredited by one of the three governing, professional Associations — the American Board for Certification in Orthotics and Prosthetics, the Board for Orthotic and Prosthetic Certification and the Board for Certification in Pedorthics. Communication and ongoing professional training are paramount in keeping Hanger at the forefront of the orthotics and prosthetics industry. Intensive educational programs, sponsored by Hanger throughout each year, help to improve the technical and patient management skills of the practitioners who work at local patient care centers. The educational programs also build camaraderie among the practitioners, and enable Hanger Prosthetics & Orthotics to efficiently train its most important assets — orthotic and prosthetic practitioners who will work directly with the patients.

Humanitarian endeavors have been of critical

importance to the Company ever since James Hanger's exemplary belief in the value of providing humanitarian aid at every possible opportunity. Those who operate the Company today participate in humanitarian aid projects on both local and global levels. In June of 2000, Hanger sent four certified practitioners to Turkey to assist Turkish earthquake amputees. During the project, the Hanger Company teamed with two non-profit organizations and with several Turkish physicians to evaluate and fit the wounded with proper prosthetic equipment. The Company hopes that by helping in Turkey and other places abroad it will not only furnish limbs for amputees, but also improve international medical standards by educating practitioners on the tenets of prosthetic care, rehabilitation and maintenance.

Locally, the humanitarian projects that the Hanger Orthopedic Group, Inc. undertakes often involve the donation of a limb to a select individual. The Company has furnished limbs and provided customized care for numerous patients throughout the country, ranging from innocent victims of drunk driving accidents to people inflicted with rare diseases. After the terrorist strikes of September 11th, Hanger offered gratis

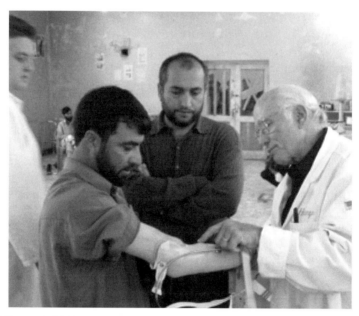

Hanger's 2002 Project First Step, was the humanitarian aid trip to Afghanistan, benefiting war ravaged amputees.

prosthetic services and products to victims in New York and Washington, D.C. In some cases, the Company's good will has been featured on talk shows like Leeza Gibbons or Sally Jessie Raphael; but, in many instances, Hanger has offered its aid without gaining publicity or recognition.

Another way the Company fulfills its responsibility of leadership in prosthetics and orthotics is the same reason the Company has been a leader from its beginning: innovation. Hanger continues to blaze new ground in the quest for superior prosthetic equipment. The advances the Company has made in recent years are of the same revolutionary caliber as those made by James Hanger when he constructed his first prosthetic limb. Now, as in the past, the Hanger Company pioneers new innovations that drastically improve the quality of prosthetics and orthotics.

One modern innovation is the Hanger ComfortFlex™ Socket System. The ComfortFlex™ Socket System is a highly contoured and flexible socket that improves the way all levels of prostheses attach to residual limbs. The old standard of socket design is often uncomfortable and causes irritation. With customized shapes and designs, the new Hanger socket system reduces socket rotation on the residual limb, and has built-in relief for concentrated pressure points, both enabling high-activity and everyday users to enjoy the benefits of more comfort and freedom. The patented system features grooves and channels that are anatomically designed with soft plastic that accommodates unique differences in muscle, bone, tendon, nerve and vascular areas from patient to patient. The result is that many amputees can control their prosthesis more effectively, allowing them to re-enter the work force and to

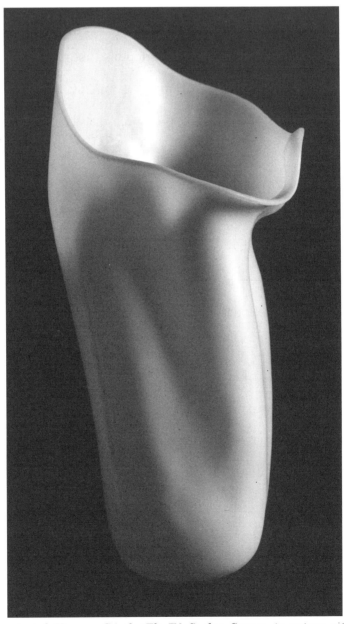

The patented Hanger ComfortFlex™ Socket System is unique with an improved, anatomically contoured design that exactly matches the underlying anatomy of the residual limb.

participate in recreational activities such as biking, running, dancing and playing golf.

Another innovation by Hanger Prosthetics & Orthotics is its Hot and Cold Sensory System, which enables amputees to sense both hot and cold environments with their prosthetic device. In a prosthetic hand, for instance, temperature sensors within the hand-shell will send signals about the temperature to a computerized circuitry system further up in the prosthetic arm. The circuitry system will interpret these signals and send new ones to electrodes on the amputee's skin. In turn, the individual will feel a sensation of hot or cold directly on his or her residual limb. Although this amazing technology to restore senses to amputees has already been invented, the Hot and Cold Sensory System is not yet available to the general public. Once the system is perfected and experimental tests completed, Hanger expects that the Hot and Cold Sensory System will make another positive impact on the prosthetics industry.

Positive impact is one fortune Hanger Orthopedic Group, Inc. cannot avoid. Whether in its unique educational programs, its humanitarian projects, or its innovative prosthetic inventions, Hanger lives up to its reputation of providing the

Team of athletes who competed at the Hanger Endeavor Games

best quality and personalized service to patients in need of prosthetic and orthotic devices. All the accomplishments of the Hanger Orthopedic Group, Inc. owe recognition to the man who set them in motion. In James Hanger's lifetime, he not only made an astounding influence on the lives of those around him, but he etched a niche in American culture and society that still exists today.

A Civil War Re-enactment

Back in Philippi, where it all began, the first days of June are much the same. Late spring rains come and disappear over the rolling wooded hills of West Virginia. The same Tygart River slices through the town; neither the town nor the river has changed much with time. Philippi today is quietly content in its secluded valley. The same families present in Hanger's age are there today, generations older, but kept together by the secrets of the wooded hills and the gurgling whispers of the winding river.

Each year, to commemorate the first land battle of America's Civil War, Philippi hosts a Blue and Gray Reunion. The festivities enthrall the townsfolk with cotton candy, bake sales, traveling one-man magic acts, bluegrass bands, arts and crafts and the battle's re-enactment. Historians from throughout the state come to debate the circumstances and strategies of the war. Anthropologists argue over the authenticity of newly discovered artifacts. Mostly, though, local families linger about in Civil War period attire, enjoying the parades and dances.

When the battle is re-enacted, the same events of early in the morning on June third, 1861 come back to life. The same group of Upshur Grays stands proudly by their new white tents. Surprise gunfire from the hill signals the Union attack. And James Hanger, whose injury is the main attraction, appears on the makeshift amputation table like he did so many years ago.

By the time of Hanger's re-enacted amputation, a large crowd gathers around his body. The young boy who plays Hanger's part grimaces oddly. His surgeon, who is really the boy's father, wears a bloody apron and fumbles through a plate of crude saws and knives. The surgeon turns his back to the audience and begins to cut. Behind him he drops bloody pieces of liver he purchased from the local supermarket the night before. Audience members cringe at this phony but gruesome trick. Fake blood splashes in the air over his shoulder. The audience throws up more sighs. By the surgery's end, Hanger's leg is gone, hidden in an illusion. Children point their fingers in awe, and the older members of the audience bare their teeth with a happy grin.

For now, that is the end of the re-enactment. Hanger becomes just another victim of a brutal war. But as the audience leaves, the surgeon and young James stand up, father and son, to finish the story. You see, they explain, James Hanger was not only the first amputee of the war, his story continues from there. He went on to make a prosthetic limb, and he even founded a company. Today that company, Hanger Orthopedic Group, Inc., has grown to be the largest and most innovative in its field.